Unspoken Resonance

Lucia H.U.

BookLeaf
Publishing

India | USA | UK

Presentation by *BookLeaf Publishing*

Web: www.bookleafpub.com

E-mail: info@bookleafpub.com

ISBN: 9789358361452

First edition 2021

To mum and dad whose love and support I sense wherever I go. To my entire family for always believing in me. To my friends for the many instances. To my mentors for guiding me and showing me how to appreciate words. To those incredible humans I come across at various times in my life for helping me find the righteous path. And to those creative souls for inspiring me to be courageous to share my own artistic expression.

1. Rebirth

My spirit was crashed,

My body weakened and my dreams
gone.

I was on earth, but I felt my soul dashed

To a different world, I was completely
gone.

I was disappointed at my surroundings,

I was upset with my innermost thoughts,

Because I felt like I was drowning

Or hurt as if I had received gunshots.

Then I slowly recognised the light within,

It was brighter than before,

I could sense healing all over my skin.

I discovered where I've been sore.

I was looking at the rebirth of my spirit,

I no longer stared at chaos or
destruction.

The pain I've felt had its limit;

I began a process of deconstruction.

It was a beginning, I could perceive.

I was tired for a long time,

But I'm now able to believe.

2. Her

Who are you? I ask.

I don't know who she is.

She seems to have fought,

I'm certain I've seen her before.

I think I know her, but it's just a thought.

I see her walking past,

The resemblance of someone familiar.

Smiling and distant, an impactful
contrast.

Her voice I recognise, faint, only a
whisper.

I think I know her, and yet I'm unsure.

Have I seen her at a forgotten place?

She's inspiring, her presence can reassure.

She's poised, with a smile she does embrace.

She observes my wounds;

She assumes I'm blameless,

I'm not, but my mistakes she eludes.

I admit my journey isn't painless.

She looks at me with caring eyes,

Can she not see I haven't been the best?

She gazes at me and cries,

She whispers, 'you need to rest'.

I see her again, not saying a word.

Who is she? I ask,

Looking at myself in the mirror.

Looking at the image blurred.

3. Silence

Silence I dreaded I welcome today.

I was once afraid of the absence of sounds;

I'm glad I've pronounced all I could say.

Quietness I sense, no one can speak.

I'm alone, I'm not afraid.

This is comfortable, this silence is unique.

I cannot hear judgment whilst I've prayed.

I embrace silence, it's now my companion.

Space between fear and my determination,

I crave calmness, I love quietness.

I'm now welcoming silence.

4. Returning

Here we are, again,

Sitting quietly,

Staring out of the window in the train,

Letting our true selves be, finally.

On the horizon train tracks are seen,

The night is all we have ahead.

The journey is short,

But this life is all we've got,

Because we surely aren't dead.

It's another trip, it's another chance to
see.

We're tired but hopeful, aren't we?

People with their phones, lost in thought.

Shutting my eyes in the inaudible carriage,

In my mind I thank those providing support.

I'm accompanied despite my baggage.

5. Distant Home

You hear the frustration,

You cannot ignore the pleads.

You no longer live in the same land

But your home is on its knees.

Injustices occur in public,

Other crimes aren't heard of.

From the far distance impotent,

The world sees the crumbling republic.

I saw that land with innocent eyes,

Now from afar I see a different place.

Hearing, reading stories, the desperate
cries,

Seeing anger on every person's face.

6. If tomorrow isn't good

Tiredness cannot be fought;

Resting is a must.

Today was exhausting,

Tomorrow might not be great.

Do we know what the future will be?

We waste our time thinking too much.

Is it pessimistic to think we're doomed?

Or is it realistic to see patterns?

Living by what's assumed.

We ruin today expecting a worse
tomorrow.

Even if tomorrow becomes worse,

Worrying now forces us to be drained.

7. Not easy to leave

Although sometimes you're in my mind,

We vanish from each other.

I know, despite our differences, you are
kind.

It wasn't easy to leave.

I'd stay, but not whilst you misbehave.

Believe me it was hard to say goodbye.

Who am I to judge? I misbehave too.

But I'm not afraid to admit mistakes.

Despising cowardice, my heart breaks.

Who am I to stay?

I miss you,

But I'd rather be away.

8. Mother

I see you in the early morning when a
warm tea awaits for me;

You're a caring woman from whom I
learn how to be.

Those long hours you've worked
showed me what is responsibility.

You put others before yourself, and do
so with immense humility.

I hear you when you say take a sweater,

The stories you tell me are something to
remember.

I cannot ignore how great your love is,
you worry about me more than you think
I know.

Mother, you strong woman of gentle
heart,

Distance nor time can ever keep us
apart.

When I smile, when I sight, when I cry,

You're in every instant I live under the
sky.

9. Destined

Time passing by,

The clock ticking,

We gotta say goodbye.

The wind blowing,

The breeze can be felt.

Are we already going?

The cards have been dealt.

Our destiny is designed,

We are certain our life is defined.

Can we alter our imperfections?

Or do we choose the burden?

Time is passing,

We keep ourselves in complete silence,

Until we start asking,

Is this what we chose?

Perhaps not.

The changes we want are close.

10. Music

I seek music when I'm feeling lonely,

When I can't find the right words,

I press play and sadness disappears
slowly.

I sense my feelings through the chords.

Whilst melodies play, I close my eyes.

I sense the beauty in every note,

The magical sounds that expand to the
skies,

The soft humming of someone's cries.

That sound that I recognise
unconsciously,

Same chord progression altering my mood;

The lyrics written honestly

Accompany me in my solitude.

11. Music is our Language

Sounds that are soothing,

I hear when I'm losing.

I listen to love songs seeking inspiration,

Finding the right words becomes a
fixation.

I hear the guitar strings being strummed,

The rhythm of a song is being drummed.

I listen to a meaningful melody,

Closing my eyes for a minute of clarity.

Notes are played, tears are shed;

When music plays everything is said.

Words and notes express all.

Music the language of the human soul.

12. This World

I know the world is different now,

We're here living without knowing how.

I would be naive to believe in normality,

But I'm not pessimistic, this isn't finality.

The world has changed,

There's so much to be explained.

We're afraid,

Our hopes and dreams seem to fade.

Wars are fought in all corners of the
world,

Many are desperate with no way to
return.

The economy crumbles,

The poorest have more struggles.

We sit quietly on our own,

Whilst somebody else fears to walk
alone.

We speak of equality,

The news reports another casualty.

We live in a world where some feel free,

Others are swimming across the sea.

Genders are the same,

Until someone is to blame.

Being a woman appears to be great,

Society tells women there's no time to
wait.

Become a mum before you're too old,

Wear tight clothes, accessorise with gold.

To be a woman seems fabulous,

But women's salaries are scandalous.

Women still get paid less than men do,

Women asking for a raise is a taboo.

Has the world changed?

Some aspects seem unchanged.

We're noticing what was already happening,

Hopefully, we're doing serious dismantling.

13. Haven't Met You Yet

To the man I will love and I haven't met yet.

Would I meet you at a sunset?

Would I meet you unaware?

Would you understand my love and care?

You don't know, but I have been confused.

Has it been love? Or have I been used?

When I see you, I'll know you're different.

It won't be your hair nor a cigarette.

It'd be the fact you'll respect me.

You won't be afraid of who I can be.

You don't know but I've cried many nights.

I've given up once, maybe even twice.

I've waited for someone as brave as you.

Someone who understands love is truth.

I know you have been broken,

All your feelings are unspoken.

I know we haven't met,

I know it's not love yet;

But if I don't say I'm waiting,

Perhaps we'll never be dating.

If I don't believe you exist,

I won't ever persist.

Acknowledging you are somewhere,

Might lead me exactly there.

14. Couldn't Conspire

Loneliness is feared,

But I'm more afraid of blurred
boundaries.

I know it's quiet,

But I preferred to be silent.

I used to trust companionships,

Until held strongly by someone's grip.

People loved me as long as I didn't
speak,

My views and comments detested
critique.

I felt lonely amongst the well dressed,

Perfect bodies, men impressed.

I felt out of place, not due to
appearance;

Their beauty and brilliance

Was not what created a distance;

It was our mere existence.

Time and convictions became evident,

We all became very negligent.

I felt out of place, discomfort I had to
face.

Conversations didn't inspire me,

I tried to explain but no one agreed.

Condoning lies didn't feel right,

Even if now I am despised.

I could feel an immense disconnection,

My mind overwhelmed of recollection.

I'm hoping my actions can inspire,

I became someone who couldn't conspire.

15. Single

Another sad look,

Someone who clearly misunderstood.

Being single isn't depressing,

I appreciate those who are caring.

Another wedding invite,

No partner nearby.

It seems lonely,

I have nothing against matrimony.

I've met men who swept me away,

Some of them have wanted to stay.

I haven't been ready to compromise

Even looking at the perfect man's eyes.

I've also been misused by heartless
men,

So I'm sure I don't want to be hurt again.

It's not fear but self preservation,

Finding true love is my expectation.

Yet single life is my paradise,

Authenticity can entice,

But it's nearly impossible to find

An honest person, patient, and kind.

Living without romance seems
upsetting,

Many couples are currently forgetting

That a partner isn't guaranteeing
affection.

Having a ring to me can be an
oppression.

Some women expect flowers,

Some men purchase them in timeless
hours;

We single women choose our own tulips

And buy them alone.

Single by choice or unable to connect,

Being on our own allows us to select

Our own unique way to grow,

To travel the roads we need to know.

16. Connection

I'd be lying if I say I don't think of you,

This is something I wish you knew.

It's not love, just affection,

I didn't confuse our connection.

It's been months since our goodbye,

I have cried but I'm alright.

You only shared your kindest words,

But we belong to different worlds.

It's sad to think we're not even friends

When our companionship transcends.

I miss a future that doesn't exist,

Your gentle kindness was a precious gift.

It's rare to perceive so much brightness,

You're one person who inspires greatness.

Despite the fact we're kilometres apart,

Your wisdom stays within my heart.

You're part of a story I did not choose,

But it's your integrity what I do not confuse.

You're part of the healing

And a new beginning.

Your accomplishments worth admiring,

Reminding me my dreams aren't expiring.

17. Nephew

Like the stars and the sun,

Young boy, you are bright.

At home your laughter is a special one.

You're curious, you're kind.

At such a young age,

You have one impressive mind.

Seeing you perceive the world

Is one of the greatest joys,

I'm amazed at all you've learnt.

Hearing you speak clearly

Amazes me every time,

You pronounce words cheerfully.

When the sun rises,

You're already smiling,

You're expecting surprises.

The brightness in your eyes

When you see a colourful sky,

Tells me you'll be wise.

18. Time and Place

I could not erase it,

Didn't want to, I admit.

The past full of memories,

It seems it's been centuries.

It's not a silver lining

But the time has gone flying.

I need somewhere to rely on,

A place to stay at dawn.

Where I went is not where I'll go,

I'm going where I can grow.

I'm here and not there,

I'm still waiting for what's fair.

The journey I imagined

Is nothing like what happened.

I wouldn't change my choices,

I'm listening to others' voices.

The pathway I've walked

Is filled with words I have thought.

There's no space for regret;

What I've said and done I have to
accept.

I could not erase it,

I don't want to forget it.

The time spent

Is now part of my present.

Who I've been

Is where I begin.

19. Now

Thoughts in my mind,

Whilst reflecting peace I find.

Slowing down I've been able to see

That all I needed is to feel free.

Looking back at the past,

Reminiscing on what couldn't last.

It's not sadness, simply admiring the
past.

I see a young woman dreaming,

Her plans and goals she's seeking.

I see optimism,

I don't see realism.

I slow down,

I hear a sound.

I hear my breath

And find my strength.

It's not easy to be conscious,

Even though I'm extremely cautious.

Our society doesn't allow

Us to live in the now.

20. Roses

Roses as red as blood,

I see petals on the mud.

I don't step on them,

I see the stem,

Has someone not noticed a flower fell?

Roses are a symbol of love,

What can they remind us of?

I think of a song that says:

'Nothing is forgotten if someone cares'.

Roses are delicate and beautiful,

People ask me who is suitable.

Like petals on the mud,

My mistakes have been judged.

Roses as colourful as they are,

They're seen not touched like a star.

I'm aware love hasn't lasted,

I know I've been distracted.

Roses blossom and wither,

Perhaps love disappeared last winter.

Every relationship needs

Attention like all seeds.

21. Arrival

I was seventeen,

I can't believe how young I had been.

I boarded a plane,

I was ready to see another terrain.

I waved goodbye,

I let my spirit fly.

I landed here;

I chose to be sincere.

I stepped on Australian soil,

I instinctively had to recoil.

But the autumn breeze

Made me feel at ease.

I was reminded

Why I was invited.

I travelled to believe,

To create and achieve.

I arrived to make a difference,

To spread joy is my preference.

I arrived at a dream place,

And wholeheartedly provide embrace.

I arrived to learn,

I am here to discern.

22. The Moon.

The colder the night feels,

The brighter the moon reveals.

A blue tint in its light,

Its radiant presence illuminates bright.

On the balcony I look up at the sky

The moon radiant isn't shy.

I wonder if it's true

That happiness is to pursue.

23. Pride

There's a fine line

Between pride and arrogance;

One can notice the sign,

Offensiveness is the evidence.

When people feel proud,

Their enthusiasm is allowed.

The arrogant is rejected,

Their attitude detested.

24. Any Given Day

I can see the sunlight

Another day to embrace

More possibilities in sight,

Uncertainty I must face.

Every day is unpredictable,

The people I meet

Their struggles not visible,

Our interactions incomplete.

I start the day with the thought

That it'll be better than yesterday,

And that more patience is brought.

I'm more accepting that not all stay.

Every instant changes me;

Every person affects my life somehow.

I'm here as I try to be,

I'm here as anyone can allow.

25. Who Bring Us Immense Peace

Friends can come and go,

Some get to stay

To see us grow,

Even if they're far away.

There are friends who depart

They are people we miss,

Death seems to keep us apart

But from time to time we reminisce.

Friends perceive us at our best and worse.

When no one else can notice our defeats,

They are present, ready to endorse.

Friends are who bring us peace.

Friends are transient,

Friends are transformative,

Friends are patient,

Friends are supportive.

Friends aren't perfect,

Friends are human too.

Friends are capable to respect,

Friends know how to say what's true.

Friends are in heaven being angels,

Friends are also warriors on this earth.

Friends get us through changes,

Friends remind us of our worth.

26. Motivation

Some days seem endless;

I wish I could explain

Why some days become restless,

And we seem to perceive pain.

There's something inside all.

We have a desire,

We have at least one goal.

We all possess a hidden fire.

When tiredness is felt,

We might want to quit,

Our fire seems to have left.

Mistakes are difficult to admit.

We tend to wait for motivation

Without making any change.

We expect inspiration

Effortlessly, isn't that strange?

27. Sydney

Sydney, you wonderful city,

Walking alongside the water

Makes me forget that I'm busy.

Living here makes me stronger.

Sydney, versatile city;

When I walk towards a park,

The view becomes pretty;

I feel my thoughts spark.

Sydney, homely city;

I call this place home every day,

Even when it's windy,

Even when the sky turns grey.

I feel like a tourist

And a local.

My love for Sydney is the purest,

Sydney to me is the most loyal.

I have cried,

I have laughed.

Sydney has seen that I've tried,

Sydney has heard when I've asked.

In Sydney I've become an adult.

Creating dreams and goals,

On some I haven't seen any result,

I haven't lost hope on some of those.

Sydney is my favourite space

I wouldn't go anywhere else.

Sydney to me is a sacred place,

Sydney is a city of beauty and nothing less.

28. The Stage

Bright lights,

Instruments untouched,

There's no one on the stage yet.

The thought of performing puts me in a
fret.

Cymbals reflecting lights

Reminding me of youthful nights.

The instruments wait to be played,

Whilst the audience waits to be swayed.

A keyboard in the corner

Reminding me I'm still a foreigner;

And whilst no one performs,

I silently wait to sing again;

Wondering if all I've done is in vain.

Guitars on the stage

Reminding me of my exact age.

I'm older,

I'm wiser.

I haven't forgotten the sounds of
nostalgia.

The bass at another corner

Reminding me I don't need an armour;

The stage is not a battlefield,

The stage is where we come to be
healed.

I'm here waiting for the dim light,

Waiting for the melodies that are right.

Whilst I wait I think that the stage

Is as surprising as turning this page.

29. Your Life

Like water to fire; you're calmness and
you wait for no one.

You've been broken, yet you love as if
no person has ever hurt you before.

You wait, you leave, you wonder what it
could be.

You're quiet, you speak, you remain
silent.

You speak for those who can't speak for
themselves;

Your voice is heard when you're not
aware.

You're peaceful like an autumn breeze,

Defending yourself with an ocean's strength;

Not letting your heart freeze.

You're radiant like sunshine

In the darkest hours.

You wait for the stars to align.

You see the colours in all flowers.

Sometimes you doubt,

You ignore your own magic.

The earth might be in drought,

Your soul rains hope, there's nothing tragic.

Your tears and words written on sand;

You feel lonely, no one has held your hand.

When there's love, no need to
compromise;

You see through every person's
disguise.

All you're searching for is a true story,

Not a romance novel, nor a tale of glory.

Simply to live the most authentic life,

With someone respecting who you are.